MY FIRST LOOK AT PETS

A GOLDEN RETRIEVER IN THE SNOW

Dogs

VALERIE BODDEN

CREATIVE EDUCATION

Published by Creative Education

123 South Broad Street, Mankato, Minnesota 56001

Creative Education is an imprint of The Creative Company

Designed by Rita Marshall

Photographs by Barbara Augello, Getty Images (Daniel J. Cox, Ghislain & Marie David de

Lossy, Tim Davis, Paul Harris, GK Hart / Vikki Hart, Yellow Dog Productions),

Sally Myers, Tom Myers

Printed in the United States of America

Library of Congress Cataloging-in-Publication Data

Bodden, Valerie. Dogs / by Valerie Bodden.

p. cm. — (My first look at pets)

Includes bibliographical references and index.

ISBN-13 : 978-1-58341-458-3

I. Dogs—Juvenile literature. I. Title. II. Series.

SF426.5.B63 2005   636.7—dc22   2005050675

First edition 9 8 7 6 5 4 3 2 1

Dogs

MAN'S BEST FRIEND

Many people call dogs "man's best friend." That is because dogs and people get along very well. People all around the world have pet dogs.

Dogs have **canine teeth** and strong legs. Most dogs have a tail. Dogs can bark, howl, and whine. They can hear and smell much better than people can.

GERMAN SHEPHERDS ARE BIG DOGS

Dogs come in many different sizes. Some dogs weigh more than 100 pounds (45 kg). Others are as small as a cat.

A dog's fur can be brown, black, white, or yellow. Or it can be a mix of colors. Some dogs have long fur or curly fur. A few kinds of dogs have no fur at all!

Dalmatian puppies are all
white when they are born.
They get black spots later.

Choosing a Dog

There are more than 200 **breeds** of dogs. Some people like big dogs for pets. St. Bernards and Great Danes are big dogs. Other people like small dogs. Jack Russell terriers, Chihuahuas (*chih-WAH-wahs*), and toy poodles are small dogs.

Active dogs make good pets for some people. Labrador retrievers, golden retrievers,

A puppy does not have
any teeth until it is three
or four weeks old.

and cocker spaniels are active dogs. They like to hunt and fetch things. Other people want calm dogs. Boston terriers and bull-dogs are calm.

Some dogs have parents from different breeds. These dogs are called "mixed breeds" or "mutts." Mutts can make good pets, too.

AUSTRALIAN SHEPHERDS HAVE LOTS OF ENERGY

Dog Care

Some pet dogs live in the house. Others live outside. Dogs that live outside should be in a **kennel**. They need somewhere warm to go when it rains or is cold.

Dogs need healthy dog food and lots of water. They need regular baths, and their fur needs to be brushed. Dogs need to have their toenails clipped. Their teeth should be brushed, too.

A DOG'S FUR NEEDS TO BE TAKEN CARE OF

CLEANING A DOG CAN BE A WET JOB

Just like kids, dogs need regular check-ups. A **veterinarian**, or vet, checks dogs to make sure they are healthy. The vet gives dogs **shots** to keep them from getting sick. Most pet dogs live 10 to 12 years.

Dog Fun

Dogs love to be near their owners. Most dogs like to be petted. Lots of dogs like to have their belly rubbed.

Some people foods,

such as chocolate and

onions, are bad for dogs.

Dogs need some exercise and playtime every day. Some dogs like to chase after their owners. Others like to swim. Most dogs like to go for long walks.

Some dogs can learn tricks. They can learn to sit up or roll over. They might learn to "shake hands." Dogs like to get a treat for doing a good job. They like to be told "Good boy" or "Good girl." Most of all, dogs like to know they are loved!

Some dogs like to serve people.

Many German shepherds

work as police dogs.

Hands-on: Doggy Tags

ID tags help people know who a dog belongs to if it gets lost. You can make an ID tag for yourself, too.

What You Need

A sheet of construction paper (any color)
Scissors
Crayons
A piece of yarn 18 inches (46 cm) long
Tape

What You Do

1. Draw a large bone on the piece of paper. Have a grown-up help you cut out the bone.
2. Write your name on the bone. Write your address and phone number, too.
3. Color the bone with fun designs.
4. Tape each end of the yarn to the bone. Then wear your new doggy tag!

IT IS A GOOD IDEA TO GIVE DOGS A TAG

Index

Words to Know

breeds—kinds

canine teeth—an animal's four longest and pointiest teeth

kennel—an outdoor pen for a dog

shots—medicines that are given through needles

veterinarian—an animal doctor

Read More

Ajmera, Maya, and Alex Fisher. *A Kid's Best Friend*. Watertown, Mass.: Charlesbridge, 2002.

Altman, Linda Jacobs. *Big Dogs*. New York: Benchmark Books, 2001.

Barnes, Julia. *101 Facts about Puppies*. Milwaukee, Wis.: Gareth Stevens, 2001.

Explore the Web

How to Love Your Dog http://www.kidsanddogs.bravepages.com

Chazhound's Free Dog Page http://www.chazhound.com/index.html

Enchanted Learning: The 50 Most Popular Dogs in the U.S.

http://www.enchantedlearning.com/subjects/mammals/dog/popular.shtml